Liturgy and Technology

Tim Stratford

Vicar of the Church of the Good Shepherd, West Derby

GROVE BOOKS LIMITED
RIDLEY HALL RD CAMBRIDGE CB3 9HU

Contents

Acknowledgements

My thanks are offered to members of DCS and GROW for their comments whilst this book was being put together and especially to its 'mentors' Trevor Lloyd and Vernon Blackmore.

'I promise to use only the forms of service that are authorised or allowed by canon law…'

The Cover Illustration is by Peter Ashton

First Impression August 1999
ISSN 0144-1728
ISBN 1 85174 409 6

1
Introduction

This booklet is written from the perspective of a priest who has lived with a computer on his desk since leaving school at the age of eighteen and who struggles to see it as anything other than a sophisticated work tool. It tries to describe Information Technology as simply a new medium in a line of varying means of communication going back to the development of the world's first written story. I believe that, as with all tools, the consequences we are faced with are not of the tool's making but due to the way it is used.

What follows is a discussion of the ways the use of computer technology can help or obstruct the normal worship of the church—especially as a result of locally produced publications replacing officially published liturgies and worship books. As with many books on the subject of worship, I will argue that we should not necessarily make use of every possible option available, that worship leaders need to be careful about the rate of change they subject worshippers to, and that the wider church needs to invest in equipping clergy and worship leaders for the new range of choices they are being faced with. I will argue the case for the particular practice of locally created seasonal service cards confined to two sides of a folded sheet with a shelf life of a number of years and for material to be drawn from sources recognized in the wider church and discussed by a group representative of the local congregation.

The *Brief History of Liturgical Publishing* in chapter 2 aims to provide a fair context for discussion, chapter 3 offers some of the practical issues that local church practitioners need to consider and chapter 4 offers some theological consideration of this. At the end is a check list that might help address the issues raised in the booklet, and a check list for those producing their own service cards. These two lists might form an agenda for discussion both in the councils of national churches and local congregations.

This booklet does not attempt to discuss the use of electronic technology during worship—sound systems, lights, video/computer projectors, interactive whiteboards and so forth. My belief is that consideration of these is best given through catalogues, demonstration and their use in live settings.

2

A Brief History of Liturgical Publishing Technology

There can be little doubt that Jesus taught his followers to pray without the need for them to resort to reading or writing and referring to complex Jewish codes. Joachim Jeremias's work in retranslating the Lord's Prayer (amongst other core gospel material) back into the probable colloquial Aramaic of Jesus results in a rhyme with two/four stress rhythm.[1] His work with that of Matthew Black on the alliteration and onomatopoeia of this clearly indicate a primarily spoken Aramaic tradition.[2] If they are right, the words of the Lord's Prayer were tightly framed and designed to be learned. This was not just a type of prayer but a form of words for the use of his followers.

Jeremias suggests that by AD 75 the Lord's Prayer was written and being used in Greek as primary teaching about prayer across the whole church—Jewish/ Christian (Matt 6.7ff), Gentile/Christian (Luke 11.1ff) and in the chatechetical material which became the *Didache*.[3]

The use of written liturgical texts continued to develop. By the time of Hippolytus of Rome (early third century) it is clear that the liturgy of the church was being set down in writing in such a way that it could regularly be referred to. The Eucharistic Prayer in The Apostolic Tradition states that a bishop has the right to pray extempore so long as it is orthodox, which Peter Cobb suggests was an indication that it was becoming stereotyped.[4]

David Hope traces the development of liturgical books through from *libelli* (small collections of Mass formulae) and sacramentaries (celebrants' books with all the necessary texts for celebrating the Eucharist) of the eighth century and which would have been in almost every church or monastery by the twelfth and thirteenth centuries.[5] The multiplication of liturgical books continued with lectionaries (Scripture readings for the Eucharist), antiphonaries (sung parts of the Mass and office), missals (combining sacramentaries, lectionaries and antiphonaries by the end of the thirteenth century), breviaries (office books) and *ordines* (instructions and directions).[6]

By the sixteenth century the early oral roots in Christian worship had developed into complex and diverse traditions perpetuated in each locality through writings which were both full of copyists' errors and took account of local ideas and customs.[7] Printing opened up the possibility of bringing order to this and

---

1   Joachim Jeremias, *New Testament Theology* (London: SCM Press, 1971) pp 193ff.
2   *ibid*, p 27.
3   *ibid*, p 195.
4   Jones, Wainwright, Yarnold (eds), *The Study of Liturgy* (London: SPCK, 1979) p 174.
5   *ibid*, p 65ff.
6   *ibid*, p 66ff.
7   Clifford Howell in Jones, Wainwright, Yarnold (eds), *The Study of Liturgy* (London: SPCK, 1979) p 241.

was used to great effect by the early reformers—and so later drove change within the Roman Catholic Church after the Council of Trent. Thus the 1570 Missal fixed the texts of the Tridentine Mass until the 1960s just as the 1662 Prayer Book fixed the Church of England's liturgies for nearly three hundred years. It would be wrong to claim that printing drove these changes but it was certainly used to some effect. Printing has not just spawned books which brought uniform order to the churches' liturgy, it has also enabled much diversity as shown by the hymn books developing out of non-conformist traditions.

In 1906 the Church of England's Royal Commission on Ecclesiastical Discipline reported that, 'the law of public worship in the Church of England is too narrow for the religious life of the present generation.'[8] The limitations of the paper media industry, however, are plain to see in recent responses to this dilemma such as the ASB, *Lent, Holy Week and Easter*, and *The Promise of His Glory*. Manuscript (with its inherent flexibility) was all that was possible for the retention of the liturgy in the fifteenth century. By the 1980s the plethora of services can barely be contained by the print medium but typescript is too laborious to be used widely across a church with a history of pre-printed services.

Patterns for Worship was published in 1995. By this time local publishing techniques had moved on considerably and become affordable. By 1998 an estimated 75% of churches were regularly using word processing.[9] Typing texts into a computer for some had become a useful investment in time as material could be stored and used again in different arrangements. Further publication of material on disk has taken a great deal of labour out of the task of producing service sheets and the possibilities have been welcomed widely.

All this could either spell a return to the confusion and potential for schism of the middle ages or it could present an opportunity for the church to meet local cultures in a way that has been lost since the likes of the *BCP* or Tridentine Mass were born. The same issues for the churches, of either using technological change as a moment of opportunity to explore new ways of being church or eventually being driven by it, pertain today as they did then.

---

8   Commentary by the Liturgical Commission on the 1980 *ASB* (London: CIO, 1980) p 10. The events that followed this statement up to the publication of the *ASB* are documented on the following pages.

9   Stephen J Mangan, *A Study of the use of the Personal Computer, and Its Applications, Within the Church of England* (BPhil Dissertation, University of Liverpool, 1998). According to this survey, although the evidence of the use of word processing was high, even in 1998 the use of the PC for worship material was insignificant in the Diocese of Liverpool compared to its use for other office work and 'Notice Sheets.' Clergy asked about its developing liturgical use responded with comments ranging from, 'I hope not,' to, 'It might replace the OHP as a means of displaying visual aids.'

3
Technological Issues

A Philosophy for Technology in Ministry

Twenty years ago, the idea of computers in the church office or minister's study was either unheard of or suggested somebody with time to spend collecting industrial scrap. The early 1980s gave birth to the IBM PC and by the end of the decade affordable clones of this (together with dedicated word-processing machines and the Apple Macintosh) were widely available. A survey of the Anglican clergy in the Diocese of Liverpool in 1989 showed 40% were using some form of personal computer, with 75% admitting to it in 1998.[10] The real assumption in 1999 is that the only ministers without a computer are those with a very well equipped secretary somewhere else in the building! This has led to a sea change in the way the church's paid ministers spend their time.

It has led to worries of clergy retreating behind the terminal screen or being seduced by the fascination of what technology can do. As time has gone by the internet, world wide web and email have offered the possibility of establishing an electronic presence in society and engaging with people without ever needing to leave the desk. Despite the worries, this seduction does not seem to have pulled the local church apart nor to have disrupted the pattern of vital face-to-face work.

What does seem to threaten much more menacingly is overwork and a mesmerizing array of choices. So much more is possible. One person can achieve a productivity beyond the capacity of a small office, printing works and accountancy company of just a generation ago. The temptation is to try to do it all. In small, under-resourced churches the minister may be the only person with access to a computer, which may itself have replaced the treasurer, the electoral roll officer, the secretary and more. When somebody resigns, the computer can do the job; this becomes the easiest option, centralization and co-ordination are attractive and it becomes the default. Most computers come with suites of software that go far beyond the normal roles of clergy and are equipped with scanners and cameras that seem to shout 'Parish Magazine' every time eyes are cast upon them. Of course the computer does not do the work but its operator does...

The technological possibilities do not have to dictate pastoral practice. Common sense can do that. The spread of IT into an increasing majority of homes also empowers the volunteer again to fulfil their roles and meet the heightening expectations associated with this.

Likewise the possibilities offered by technology do not have to dictate liturgical practice. There are many other factors that can do this. But technology does open doors that have not been open before. Some it is wise to enter; others it may not be.

10 Mangan, *op cit.*

Masters and Servants

Everybody who works behind a computer screen needs to be sure that they remain the master of the work and do not let the technology take over. It is easy to become a fundamentalist to new types of working practice: why spend an age trying to use a scanner and word processor to manipulate an image into just the right place on a service sheet when it would be quicker to use scissors and glue? It may be a personal learning exercise (which should make things much quicker and more convenient next time) but if it becomes a persistently slow way of working, remember that the older technology still works!

Similar rules about the use of time might apply to the production of regular service sheets in most churches: should the hymns be typed out in the right place week in and week out, what about responses to intercessions, variations to shape and content of the liturgy, the collect of the day and the readings? There are strong arguments in favour of tailored service sheets each week—in particular in relation to their accessibility to newcomers—but just because it is possible does not mean that it is always the right thing to do. In some places this may be right, especially where there are large numbers of visitors on a regular basis and where there is a substantial secretarial resource. But this is not everywhere. In most places a tailor-made service sheet is a great help on special occasions but not every week.

Alongside the logistical problems, much of the theological discussion in Chapter 4 argues against a constantly-changing printed liturgy. When everything is committed to paper separately for each worship occasion, the potential for spontaneity and freedom seems further diminished, identity with the wider church may seem more tenuous and the congregation may be less able to worship without their eyes forever scanning the service sheet at every twist and turn. In many parishes the existence of a lay/ordained 'Worship Committee' has been a powerful force in the sensitive renewal of liturgy. Such collaboration is completely disempowered where things change every week. They simply cannot keep up or shape what is happening.

But technological advance can offer advantage which does not have to become an obstacle for worship.

New Flexibilities

The introduction of the ASB offered limited new flexibility to the celebration of Communion in the Church of England in 1980. In the main text there were options for the confession to be said during the preparation or after the intercessions; there were four Eucharistic Prayers, and later two Lord's Prayers. The appendices offered three alternative confessions, alternative orders for the intercessions, an alternative prayer of humble access, and much more that presidents themselves may use. This was needed by the church but was clumsy in a book. It led to uses of the liturgy that never necessarily had any considered rhyme or reason (such as rotating Eucharistic prayers irrespective of other factors—Prayer One on the first Sunday of the month, Two on the second and so on). It also meant that the material in the appendices was difficult for congregations to access—

'Now turn to page 166…' This meant good material was under-used. On the good practice side many churches developed a seasonal variation in the placing of the confession, using one option in the penitential seasons and another for the rest of the year.—though even making this provision within the limitations of a book meant congregations needing to learn when to skip pages and when not to.

Application of some of these lessons in the new era of desk-top publishing and inexpensive printing show how technology helps. For instance, having different service sheets for Advent, Lent and the rest of the year can take account of alternative forms of confession, and there may be seasonal variety of the Eucharistic Prayers or seasonal sentences. 'Alleluia! Christ is risen' does not need printing on the Lenten Commuion card.

Patterns for Worship lends itself to this usage, but with care. Limiting its use and limiting the possibilities that new technology offers to seasonal blocks through the year has the potential both to strengthen the contours of the year's shape and to prevent too rapid a pattern of change for congregations. Worship committees ought to be able to grapple with this array of new services and may be able to contribute a great deal to their production. With sensitive layout, 'ordered' structure and mooring to unchangeable pillars in the service (such as the Lord's Prayer) locally produced seasonal service cards can open to churches the richness of modern liturgical diversity without casting everything adrift.

At the Good Shepherd, a Liverpool UPA outer estate church, this seasonal approach has been adopted. The first service produced was for ordinary Sundays of the year—on green card naturally. One choir member who was anxious about increased flexibility slapped the service card down on his stall loudly during the notices as it was introduced and said, 'I'm not having this!' or words to that effect. This first draft of the 'green card' was a very conservative editing out from Rite A of the normally unused options during summertime. The major difference for people was that they had no pages to keep skipping over and it did not have a glossy red cover. It also did not have the Eucharistic Prayer printed in full. After his first experience of using the card, our choir leader publicly apologized and said that had he known that was all it was about he would have been quite happy. The church was already in the habit of using other material from *Patterns for Worship*, the Iona Community and others without it ever being printed for the congregation. The small selection of service cards they now have has enabled this material to be used more easily and appropriately by them without fuss or irritation and with the Worship Committee able to offer serious consideration of each one.

Even still, such limited use of new technology needs clear strategic thinking by the church at all levels.

Cost, Waste and Ecology

In 1891 John Stainer wrote, 'The inconvenience and costliness of the number of separate books usually requisite for the members of a Choir, in the performance of an ordinary Choral Service, have long pointed to the desirableness of a manual which should, as far as possible, unite under one cover all that is necessary for the choral rendering of, at least, those portions of the Church's Services which are less liable to variation.'[11] Technological change has dealt inconvenience and costliness of separate books a fatal blow. Indeed for John Stainer's purposes, copyright law aside, the photocopier and stapler probably did that. But the disposability of locally printed material still makes it desirable to have manuals which unite under one cover. Undoubtedly the Church of England is still going to have to produce some form of beautifully bound and gold-blocked book to satisfy this, though its usefulness for Sunday worship may not be a significant factor in its sales.

This resonates with an instinctive sense that there seems to be something wasteful in producing sheets and cards that are not intended to last for ever. In these increasingly ecologically sensitive times wastefulness may be opposed to the church's mission and message and it would be wrong for the church to organize its liturgy such that stewardship revolved around keeping the paper cabinet well stocked.

It was once naively hoped that the electronic office would be the saviour of the world's paper forests. How wrong can you be! It might have taken somebody with a typewriter months to work through a ream of paper; with a modern computer it can be done in a day, or in less than five minutes on an inexpensive Risograph printer. A great deal of this is waste and unnecessary. It is work represented on paper that has value, not the paper itself. Now that the work is so easily repeatable on another sheet of printer paper, the paper is consumed as if it has no cost. Christians who care that this might be costing the earth will inevitably be seriously concerned about churches casting a ream of paper or card into the bin at the end of every service. A seasonal approach to printing new liturgies and the intention that such liturgies might last for a number of years is a way to address this. In a poor church it also makes the exercise affordable.

The ASB has 1296, A5 printed pages. If this were produced as a Sunday service sheet that is enough for 324 A4 folded service sheets or 16 a year for twenty years. Among these pages are the propers for the Blessing of an Abbott (not needed in many parishes) and much other material not used nearly so often as seasonal eucharistic rites might be. Modern technology does seem to produce a great deal of waste but it does not have to. Appearances can be deceptive and users may have more to do with the waste than the technology itself—technology just makes it possible. Alternative responses to this are to use an OHP or the likes of *Visual Liturgy* 2.0 which can drive a computer projector directly.

Sticking to the Rubrics

Books have a uniformity about them. An ASB bought in Truro is likely to be the same as one bought in Newcastle. When churches buy service books the one held in the hand of a minister leading the service is usually the same as the ones

---

11 Sir John Stainer, Editor's Preface to *The Cathedral Prayer Book* (London: Novello and Company Ltd, 1891).

the congregation have. It has been the practice of the Church of England to print the rules determining what it is lawful to do and what not in these books. These rules used to be in red for those prosperous enough to buy colour versions of the *Book of Common Prayer*, hence the term 'rubric.' In posh versions of the ASB they are blue. On locally produced service cards they tend not to exist at all. There may be instructions printed in italics for the congregation, but not normally the requirements of the wider church. Even where shape, order and the wording of the liturgy are changed there is not necessarily any indication of this. When once the congregation might have policed the degree to which their ministers played fast and loose to the liturgy, now that relies on their memory of what the books used to say—a memory that could, no doubt, fade.

When the ASB was first introduced many churches found it difficult to use and those with resources planned to print their own shorter versions. Some traditions within the church found that the material they wanted to use often was inaccessible in appendices, so they too planned their own versions. It was an expectation in the Liverpool diocese, as no doubt in many others, that printer proofs of all such proposals be sent to the Bishop for approval. It was quite appropriately part of his requirement that no rubric was omitted or changed. These productions were only undertaken by very few well resourced churches and were meant to last for years. The scale of the approval task was within the scope of already heavily worked diocesan officers. Technological change now means this is no longer the case.

The Roman Catholic Church has developed an innovative approach that wholeheartedly embraces IT. Their liturgy is made available in electronic form on a CD-ROM and is inseparable for most users from software which enforces the rubrics. It even knows the date, and if a service is intended for Lent it will not let you have the Gloria. The ethos of the Church of England and many other churches is different from this. Local innovation is valued to varying degrees. Clergy live under a more relaxed rule with a greater degree of autonomy. Local congregations, whilst valuing their association with the wider church, do not like to consider themselves controlled by it.

For churches which try to honour local expression yet provide for a recognizable degree of commonality, there may be no technological fix. Those who try to hold back the tide like King Canute may drown in a sea of change. Technology is here and progresses, whether churches like it or not. Enforcement of rules will not be possible unless a large professional police force is employed.

What is essential for such churches is to ensure that their liturgical material is easily available in computer-friendly form. Through the laws of copyright which are now being strengthened over the World Wide Web in Europe the integrity and completeness of material can still be ensured. Through Continued Ministerial Education, and with trust, wise use of it with an eye to long term Christian formation of congregations can be encouraged. Templates and prefixed sample services can be offered showing good practice and making it easier to follow the rules than break them.

The *Visual Liturgy* program makes service sheet production easy for many people who do not get on well with their word processor or desktop publisher. Version 2.0 has similar features to the RC disk including being able to work out the liturgical season from the computer's date, but it is not as prescriptive. Whilst it is not easy to tailor page breaks and line spacing without importing the results into desk top publishing software, it makes assembling the liturgy from an outline level through to the printed words very easy. It encourages users to think about both shape and content of a service. (It does not require a desk top publisher or word processor to be used in conjunction with it, and it can even create paperless worship by driving a computer projector directly.) It provides a readily available vehicle on which templates and sample services can be published and the Church of England already does this in a limited way. Sample services may be tinkered about with, but many users would no doubt value the templates and use them without change. If what is professionally published is good and easy to use this will be the most well trodden track. Why not incorporate coaching notes too —rubrics for information if not for enforcement? Most leaders in churches are not anarchic.

The Law

Copyright law is already directly applicable to electronic publishing and in 1999 was considerably strengthened across Europe to be enforceable among internet serviceroviders (ISPs). It is actually a breach of copyright for somebody to store material on a computer they do not have permission to. Those who produce local service sheets need to be sure they respect copyright and where they have permission to reproduce material should be careful to reproduce the appropriate copyright notice too. *Visual Liturgy* 2.0 will automatically generate these notices for material it knows to be copyright. Most liturgical publishers make the form of such a notice clear in their publication and for Church of England liturgies a leaflet is available called *A Brief Guide to Liturgical Copyright*.[12] It is illegal to reproduce most modern hymns and songs without paying a fee either separately to the publishers or through a wide-ranging licence.

Church laws such as the Worship and Doctrine Measure have applicability no matter what publishing format is being used. In the Church of England the issue is not whether the rules exist but whether they are followed. Use of computers might make it easier to ignore the rules and maybe more likely that some rules will be ignored. But it does not change them. In the new climate this can heighten the importance of consensus being achieved. There will always be some who flout the rules. If the majority are flouting the rules, it may be that the rules are wrong.

Church laws do enable many worshippers to gather in the security that their

---

12 *A Brief Guide to Liturgical Copyright* is published by the CBF and is available from Church House Bookshop, Great Smith Street, London, SW1P 3BN. CBF also published a booklet in 1994, *Liturgical Texts for Local Use*, in which conditions for reproduction are also set out. This will soon be superseded by a more comprehensive 'Praxis' publication.

spiritual openness in church is not going to be abused or mistreated. Without such security it may be harder to be open. Rules about worship also determine much of the spiritual formation of the worshippers. That a church reflects on this strategically and seek consensus offers it a great opportunity—not necessarily a threat. If there is no consensus in a church and among its leaders about these things, technological change applied to liturgy may create anarchy. But it also brings the church to a moment in history when a wide consensus is more significant than the enforcement of a practice drawn up in a smaller circle. God does not seem to share the human fear of many institutions in moving from the exercise of control to the exercise of trust. Nor should the gospel community.

Design and Pictures

There was one picture in the *Book of Common Prayer* (crest—inside front cover—CUP editions at least) and none in the ASB. They often dominate locally produced service sheets. A picture can be worth a thousand words yet it is not always clearly thought through what the messages might be. A great deal of thought, creativity and debate in church structures is given to the patterns of word and movement in worship and indeed to the appearance of the final publications in book form, but little guidance is given for local service sheets.[13] Typesetting and pictures can make very powerful statements.

We are now in a visual culture and respond to pictures, yet liturgical formation often concentrates on words, giving no guidance to the dominant medium of the age and because no guidance is given ministers may assume anything goes. As well as pictures, layout and typography give a feel to the words that are used. Try printing out the same service both in the ASB's 'Palatino' font and in something like the child-like 'Kids' font to see the effect.

It would be folly to believe that the options could ever be limited through enforcement, or even that this might be desirable, but guidance could be offered. Far from being read as a challenge to autonomy, many local ministers might welcome that guidance. Within the Church of England the urge to show, in the local context, that the church belongs to the whole seems very strong. When Rite A Communion was first published in a separate book, it set a style. Many churches which decided to print their own customized versions still did so between shiny red covers. It would be perfectly possible to set a style for local service cards to follow as a demonstration of their identity with the wider church to which the local one belongs. This is done for books and web sites. If the styles were carefully published for *Visual Liturgy* and popular word processors and desk top publishers (either as documents or in the form of guidance notes), those working on local service sheets would be all the better resourced. Most clergy do not understand DTP in the way that professional publishers do. It would be perfectly easy to design common forms of subheadings, main text, rubrics and so on, which help

---

13 Some discussion of the most important issues is offered in *Patterns for Worship* p 236 and *Liturgical Texts for Local Use.*

give congregations the right sorts of cues as they read and offer a common typographic language.

It is doubtful as to whether the level of specification of this should be as tightly bound in many churches as the Roman Catholic Church has chosen for its Liturgy Disk. Here even the line breaks in prayers cannot be altered to fit the constraints of pages. Often fitting a service onto the four pages of a single folded sheet is a trade off against the integrity of poetic line structure that churches in non-book cultures would want to make for the sake of simplicity in the final product. A card which just has a front, a back and an inside can be much more comfortable for some people than having to watch out for page numbers.

The debate about whether there should be a common language of pictures or a recognizable symbolic framework across any particular church is not so easy. The older technologies of publication have barely ever addressed this. Within the Church of England and the Roman Catholic Church a number of the religious orders have been addressing it especially as Information Technology has made publication of their work easier. The material is often of a very high quality, for instance the work from Tovey Abbey or St Paul's Multi-Media, much of which is published to fit with the Common Worship Lectionary. Magazines like CPAS's *Church Leadership* also distribute clip art (and the internet is awash with it) but this does not have the common identity or integrity to it that the religious orders have achieved. Although this work is easily available through these private enterprises, at present its use and impact is not being discussed widely. This might be encouraged and may even lead to some forms of artwork being distributed alongside churches' official material as an easy resource which, if widely used, could benefit the churches' identities.

Definability and Authoritativeness

When faith was conveyed through oral tradition its authorities were those who knew the stories. When religious truths were committed to writing things did not change very much: the learning required to read and write, coupled with the value of manuscript books, limited the number of those who could claim to be authorities. Printing and the Reformation began a change though physical books still obey the laws of nature and are limited in accessibility by space and time. Electronic publishing is amorphous and access to texts is so widespread it is no longer linked to authority. However, this is no argument against the church publishing material it believes is authoritative in this media.

The internet can seem to blur the boundaries of truth though in fact it does not. A publication on CD ROM is as defined and unchangeable in just as limited a way as the contents of a book. Literacy is changing. Once it was the size of infrastructure required to communicate through print or broadcast that commanded authority. If society is to continue to need to know what authority something carries, the signs are still there to be read, even on the internet, and they will be read as well, for instance, as the authority that different titles of newspaper carry today. Some of the clues are different and only just emerging; some are as they always have been. A significant investment in a high quality web site gets respect. Better that churches publish their material openly under their own ownership on the web and CD ROM, where the right signals are given and it can easily be found without adulteration, than that it only be available through third parties and open to their editorial license.

A Virtual Church

Some commentators argue that western society is changing such that locality is ceasing to matter, yet even the greatest multi-media virtual experience will never be as vital as the real thing. Emails, even telephone or video conferencing, are no substitute for the interaction that takes place when human beings meet face to face. Churches which are communities where people interrelate as full human beings cannot be replaced by the electronic community. But perhaps the church should be present in electronic society as well.

Publishing liturgical and devotional texts in digital form as a service to local churches brings with it a new set of issues the church must face, but establishing a presence in the computerized world of the information super highway is quite different again. This is not just a channel through which information is exchanged, it is a place of remote encounter with other people; it is a busy and crowded place; it is a place which carries news, gossip and stress; a place in which people can become absorbed for an age. If churches are going to make their presence known in this space it should not just be about information and news. Like many church buildings do, the church in cyber space should convey something of the numinous presence of God. Maybe this is done by a virtual walk around St Paul's Cathedral,[14] maybe it should also be done in liturgical and ritual ways. Prayer web sites and prayer 'chat rooms' exist, but there must be a great deal more that can be done which touches the spirit. This is probably more rightly work that can be done by individuals and local churches than central church structures. If this is going to be encouraged those central church structures may also need to ensure that they offer links to their parishes as experiments are made and lessons learnt. Maybe they should even consider resourcing those churches to enable them to produce creditable web sites.

Local churches which engage in this world need to be mindful that following Christ is more about human encounter and the nature and quality of relationships than it is about anything else. Surely they should be honest to their rootedness in particular places and should reflect their context—to do anything else would not be honest to humanity. Even web surfers are not supra-contextual.

14 www.stpauls.london.anglican.org

4
Theological Issues

A Living Corporate Affair?

In his book *Liturgy and Liberty*, John Leach writes about the difficulty of turning liturgy into worship.[15] Worship does not happen on paper but when people give time to draw near to God. Liturgy is not so much about the setting down of printed words as the use of shared material and the ordering of time so that people can worship in confidence alongside each other. It is primarily about corporate events. Even the use of the daily office by many clergy on their own is about drawing near to God alongside others. Although this may not be at the same time and in the same place as each other, the use of common prayers, canticles and readings is felt to be shared.

At the national level within the Church of England the tension between the cold and sometimes individual writing and reading of liturgical texts against worshipping with them has been explicitly realized. In preparing the new Common Worship material, the experience of the use of early versions by 800 formally appointed 'experimental parishes' has been an important part of the process. Members of the House of Bishops have also been encouraged to use the material in worship before they form judgments on it at their desks or in committee. The experience is not altogether new. Across Europe during the Reformation, ideas about worship, and new texts setting those ideas out, were in a constant state of flux, changing through new experiences and learning.

If freedom to choose from shared material within a huge canon and the ordering of its use is passing from the wider church to the local, so too a great deal of responsibility is changing hands. Whilst the wider church may reserve some limitations to the shape and content of local services to preserve the sense of congregations being part of a greater body,[16] it gives more possibilities for the ordering of worship than ever will be tested out. Those who work at word processors producing liturgies for use in local churches are much closer to the congregations who will use that material in worship. They will most often live in the same local context and share the histories of their communities. They will be co-worshippers with those congregations. The way the prepared liturgy helps or hinders actual worship should be seen in a much more connected way than a broad church at its national level could ever hope. As long as the need to test these connections is realized as well at the local level as it is in the wider church, the quality of gathered worship events as corporate living affairs can only benefit.

---

15 John Leach. *Liturgy and Liberty* (Eastbourne: MARC. 1989) p 13ff.
16 Even the 'Service of the Word.' which gives the greatest flexibility of any authorized Church of England service. includes a great deal of prescription to this end. The service is not 'anything goes' as many have said. it is simply less prescriptive than anything else the Church has produced. See *Patterns for Worship* (London: CHP. 1995) p 13ff, especially p 18.

But this will not happen best if these connections are made simply by clergy and worship leaders themselves based on how they 'feel it went.' Worship as a corporate and living affair is not just about the moment itself—it should also lead people on. And it is not just about how it felt to the leader—things can seem very different when you are the one being led. Local churches need to make sure that they find space for dialogue over time about the quality of their worship and can monitor it by signs of growth and maturity.

It is not easy to sit in front of a computer screen (or over a typewriter) and assemble words that you hope are going to lead other people into worship. Ministers and worship leaders who believe that national liturgies do not fit as well with the church in their context as those which are locally produced will need to approach their task with humility and sensitivity as much as with creativity.

Empowerment or Disempowerment?

Amid the tangle of rules and ceremonies belonging to the Pharisees, Jesus taught his followers, 'You should pray like this: Our Father...'[17] In this Jewish context, complication disabled their prayer and simplicity gave it new possibilities. Yet those who have a professional or religious life in which there is a great deal of time given over to disciplined prayer can often thrive on sophisticated patterns. Jesus passed no judgment on this except where it provoked arrogance—the spirituality of others being judged in a way that diminished them.

It is very easy for the professional to introduce too much complexity into the liturgies that others are expected to worship with and it is not always apparent when this has happened. The disempowered do not always feel adequate enough to say so either—crowds congratulated the emperor on his fine dress...

The liturgies of the wider church, used over decades, may have the weakness that they do not connect with every context equally well in a world where we increasingly realize and value different shades and textures of life. But they have been loved and well worshipped with, not least because of their familiarity. A new service sheet every week may provide great opportunity to connect with every twist and turn of a community's life, but it can also be pharisaic in its complexity and make it impossible for people who are seeing it for the first time to worship.

Even for the highly literate, it is difficult to pray to God when you are not sure what you are praying about until the end of the prayer. Reading ahead while speaking an unfamiliar prayer does not help the spirit. 20–25% of the working-age population of Britain overall have poor literacy skills.[18] In some congregations the number will be much higher, and here the set liturgies of the wider church are also felt to be least appropriate and in need of local adaptation. It can be hard for ministers whose formation leads to a very sophisticated approach to worship, and who are comfortable with a varied and wide diet to identify with

---

17 Matthew 6.9.
18 International Adult Literacy Survey: 1997.

the bafflement that congregations might be left with coping with new liturgies too often. The gospel demands that all Christian people be enabled through their spiritual disciplines to pray better, not bemused by the tastes of professionals.

Christian Formation Through Liturgy

The Church of England holds its doctrine to be wrapped up in its worship.[19] This is wise recognition that it is through their worship that the people of God grow in their understanding of their faith. Whilst we may learn a great deal about living lives of faith outside of corporate worship, it is here that we reflect and make sense of this.

Carolyn Headley, in her Grove booklet on *Liturgy and Spiritual Formation*,[20] suggests four ways in which worship is formative to spiritual development: encounter; learning the faith; developing an integrated life; and learning to live in the love of Christ. Such positive formation does not happen automatically and in her book she offers four panels of practical suggestions to develop things.[21] Indeed, sometimes worship can be used as a tool of containment or oppression.[22]

Learning the faith is particularly dependent on liturgical texts such as creeds, prayers, lectionaries. Beyond their use, study of these may even be a means to deeper understandings of the faith.[23] Developing an integrated life is dependent on a rhythm of prayer being encouraged and on worship being ordered to give opportunity for reflection and challenge.

Local worship leaders who find themselves taking on more responsibility for the ordering of worship need to realize the formative responsibility they have. Whilst a narrow selection of texts may limit learning, constant change with no consistency can confuse and create equal dependency.

Authority and Order Against Permission to Innovate

The 1662 *Book of Common Prayer* was published as part of the process of Charles II's restoration to the throne and as such was part of his nation-building.[24] The liturgy of most churches does not carry such political significance today but still there are interests in the churches (and the Church of England is no exception)

---

19 According to Canon A5 the doctrine of the Church of England 'is to be found in the Thirty-nine Articles of Religion, The Book of Common Prayer and the Ordinal.'

20 Carolyn Headley, *Liturgy and Spiritual Formation* (Grove Worship Series No 143, Cambridge: Grove Books Ltd, 1997).

21 *ibid* pp 15, 20, 23 and 27/8 respectively.

22 *eg* E P Thompson, *The Making of the English Working Class* (London: Penguin, 1988).

23 Carolyn Headley, *op cit*, p 20.

24 The second paragraph of the Preface begins, 'By what undue means, and for what mischievous purposes the use of the Liturgy came, during the late unhappy confusions, to be discontinued, is too well know to the world, and we are not willing to remember. But when, upon his Majesty's happy Restoration it seemed probable, that, amongst other things, the use of the Liturgy also would return of course unless some timely means were used to prevent it; those men who under the late usurped powers had made it a great part of their business to render the people disaffected there unto, saw themselves in point of reputation and interest concerned with their utmost endeavours to hinder the restitution thereof...*(Bracketed sections omitted.)*

who rightly have power in their authority over its ordering. This is not least the case for bishops as they seek to be a focus for unity. The possibility of diverse local liturgical traditions can, at first thought, appear to be at odds with this.

History shows that the way people worship is not a single given thing for all people in all times. It needs to be different from place to place and for each age. The *Book of Common Prayer's* preface itself says both, 'according to the various exigency of times and occasions, such changes and alterations should be made therein, as to those in Authority should from time to time seem either necessary or expedient' and, '…in men's ordinances it often chanceth diversely in divers countries.' This seems not to be a contentious thing until that cultural diversity demands liturgical diversity across a church used to operating as a single organizational entity. Only then do we consider unity to be under threat.

There are all sorts of ways that worship demonstrates cultural differences despite the liturgies used—through the music, the architecture, the symbolism, the identities of the ministers and leaders, the movement and the nature of the preaching. There are often ways in which these things require the liturgy to be adapted too for integrity's sake. It is potentially more at odds with the unity of the whole church for local congregations to run counter to an authority that demands uniformity than it is to live within a broad provision which the whole church can accept as orthodox.

It is precisely this that *Patterns for Worship* attempts to do, particularly in making authorized provision for churches which were already using liturgical forms which the wider church had not otherwise formally approved, *eg* in some Urban Priority Areas and in the Family Services of a great swathe of churches.[25] Technology opens the door of possibilities much wider than the limitations of the Service of the Word published in *Patterns for Worship*. Local ministers and worship leaders within a church which proclaims its doctrine through its liturgy must be sure they are familiar with the degree of choice they are given if those in authority are to have confidence that the church's integrity as a whole is not threatened. This demands that the liturgical formation of the clergy in a church like the Church of England be taken far more seriously than perhaps was needed when the worship books presented givens.

Of course the reasonable limitations that authority and order can demand may prevent the innovation the church needs if it is to learn. Innovation has never required a computer. Innovators will experiment whatever the rules of the church. Churches need to be sure they can continue to value this work and the more the boundaries are drawn for fear of a computer-led anarchy the less space may be made for new learning.

Localness and Catholicity

Beyond the issue of authority and unity is the age-old tension between localness and catholicity which is felt within many congregations. We need to proclaim our

---

25 *Patterns for Worship* pp 2–3.

universal faith (not a distortion) but in terms that resonate with local experience. If local liturgies are to be produced it should be for this very reason.

If one of the marks of an emerging postmodern society is a rejection of old authorities and the personal freedom to 'pick and mix,' it might seem that 'pick and mix liturgies' connect with the mood of the time. But who will do the picking and mixing? Mark Santer writes, 'The church's liturgy is a drama which is not the private property of any particular individual or group. It is the common possession of the whole people of God. We are not free simply to make up the texts and actions. At the same time, if our celebrations are not to be merely antiquarian, the texts, the stage-directions and the staging must always be open to renewal and adaptation in response to the constraints of the historical, social and physical situation of each particular community...It is the task of liturgists, both experts and practitioners, to enable believers to experience themselves here and now as one people of God. The texts are important. As with all poetry, there must be a proper precision of word and image. Place, setting and ritual are important. Liturgy, like all drama, is more than a matter of reading words. It is an event in time and space.'[26]

This is the theology and understanding of mission that underlies much of the world-wide Anglican Communion's liturgical renewal breaking free from the *BCP*. Dinis Sengulane is a bishop in Mozambique and writes, 'When liturgy takes into account children, the young, adults, the old, the departed, spiritual beings (whether regarded as angels or demons), rain and environment, national leaders, heaven and hell, houses and fields, colour and movement, gestures and symbols, then it is dealing with the concerns of African peoples, as it builds up the worship of God, Father, Son and Holy Spirit.'[27]

Dinis Sengulane writes with the perspective of a continent. Desktop publishing makes this same exercise possible for a housing estate. Those who engage in it at such a small local level must be sure not to cast loose their moorings to a tide of 'anything goes' but be sensitive to the connections their neighbourhood naturally makes with the kingdom of God, so strengthening them.

Individualism and the Worship of the Laos

Mark Santer (above) writes that 'the worship of the church is not the private property of any individual or group.' A church whose liturgy is produced and authorized through the collaborative processes of central decision-making bodies in dialogue with local congregations can avoid the dangers of an individual's limited vision. Where a large part of the task of liturgical authorship is passed to local ministers this may not be so. Congregations have always been at the mercy of their clergy in terms of their collaborative or individualistic style but at the end of their day liturgies such as those in the ASB could truly be held to be shared

26 Mark Santer, 'The Praises of God' in Michael Perham (ed), *Liturgy for a New Century* (London: SPCK/Alcuin Club, 1991).

27 Dinis Sengulane, 'An African Perspective,' in Kenneth Stevenson and Bryan Spinks (eds), *The Identity of Anglican Worship* (Pennsylvania: Morehouse Publishing, 1991) p 161.

because of the process by which they came into being. This may no longer be so to the same extent.

The creation of liturgies for worship services in local churches is not as new to the church of God as it is to the Church of England. But part of the nature of the Church of England has been in the way the individuality of local clergy has limited expression because of the shared expectation of the form of worship (in most places most of the time). If this has theological merit,[28] then guidelines or even new powers for PCCs might help balance the power that the worship leader has over a congregation through the word processor produced worship sheets. It may also behove the more cautious ministers and worship leaders to be sure they work collaboratively lest they abuse this power.

Evolution and Constant Changing

The world just does not seem to stay the same. It is quite unsettling but it appears to be a creation ordinance and part of God's design.

J D Benoit, reflecting on the liturgical renewal of the French Reformed churches as an open and moving tradition in the 1950s wrote quite beautifully and in typical French style:

> The liturgy, then, cannot be simply a return to the past. It does not develop artificially and arbitrarily; it is a living, growing organism, a tree which develops and is always sending out new shoots. The liturgy is an uninterrupted stream, a living spring of prayer throughout the centuries, sustaining the prayer of the church and our own individual prayers. To this great river of liturgical life, which is one with the stream of Christian life itself, we must continually be returning, so that our liturgies do not become little streams at its margins which soon lose themselves in sterile backwaters.[29]

Service books in many churches (especially those books with 1296 pages) represent a great investment and encourage people to fix tradition such that it fits the books. (This probably is not the only human trait that leads us to want to fix tradition!) Local production of service cards and inexpensive modern printing methods represent nothing like this scale of investment for either local or national churches. This seems to offer great opportunity to churches that want to run with the changes we live with year by year. It only threatens those traits within us that enjoy the comfort of what we know.

Eyes Down

Perversely, the limitations of familiar prayers and forms of liturgy allow the human spirit to wander more freely, to sense fellowship with others worshipping alongside, to share with them the symbols and drama drawing them into fellow-

---

28 The letters of John, for instance, say much about the importance of what is shared in the church over and against the style of individuals. Diotrephes is particularly singled out as a church leader to beware of (3 John 9).

29 J D Benoit, *Liturgical Renewal: Studies in Catholic and Protestant Developments on the Continent* (London: SCM Press Studies in Ministry and Worship, 1958).

ship with God. Fresh liturgies draw attention back to the words and keep the eyes pinned to the paper lest one puts a foot wrong or speaks out of turn. The drama of a live event tells a story in which the worshipper is moved on. Eyes fixed on a card or book can be constantly rehearsing what has gone before and looking at what is next. Congregations bound week by week to this activity are led into a more individualistic experience of church than those whose hands and eyes are freed.

Two observations follow. First: fresh liturgies can be predictable. There is much experience, especially in UPA churches, of only printing a bare minimum of material on cards yet still enabling people to take part. For instance, the intercessions in *Patterns for Worship* can be used, despite their varying responses, without any words being on a card for people. For example,

We pray for God's grace, saying:
Lord, receive our praise:
and hear our prayer.
Lord, receive our praise:
and hear our prayer.

People catch on without having to think. Week by week this way of learning a response gets even more familiar.

Second: change every week is disruptive. The following chapter suggests an approach to using material which connects well with changes through an annual cycle and gives time for the rhythm of such changes to become second nature.

And Finally: Corporate Identity

It has been said that the little red book (ASB Rite A Communion booklet) gave a sense of corporate identity to the Church of England and that page 119 presented a visual image in the mind that gave worshippers a sense of belonging wherever they were.[30] This was probably true, but it hardly bears significance as a theological principle by which the future direction of the liturgy of the church might be governed. Nevertheless 'corporate identity' is a tool organizations can use to help people recognize them and have a sense of belonging. Rather than worrying about the loss of the ASB in the Church of England, a theology of the denominational logo and the copyright notice at the end of locally produced service sheets might serve the churches well.[31]

---

30 An observation made by Stephen Sykes at a Praxis Consultation 'Liturgy and Computers' January 1995, St Matthew's, Westminster.
31 Although this is written slightly tongue in cheek it is an issue that has had to be addressed. Newly authorized material in the Church of England is soon to be published on the official web site in such a way that when it is downloaded it will come in a recognizable style.

5
The Choices

The fact is there is no choice about whether churches work with information technology or not. It is a firm feature of our world, it is not going to diminish in importance and it is going to change the way life has been lived (at least in 'western' nations) dramatically—if it has not done so already. Churches need to consider how they are going to live with this.

Ignoring it is not a realistic option. In most churches, to control the use of computers would be a radical departure from the way that discipline has been exercised previously. To be uncritical about the changes which we are faced with is unnecessarily naive.

Those who publish worship material for the church are going to be under increasing pressure to do so in the most accessible electronic forms.

- For those who must earn their living by selling the material, CD ROM is the most reliable route for the time being. This will be joined by the internet when e-commerce and copyright issues are solved.

- Material that is to be placed freely in the public domain needs to be placed on the internet in identifiable official locations which can be trusted. Either under File Transfer Protocol rather than Hyper Text Transfer Protocol (as this helps maintain the integrity and completeness of what is downloaded), or with digital signatures which protect the identity of texts and images regardless of their storage location.

- In this new world, consensus may be the only viable means of encouraging common practice. Work and energy needs to be invested within our varied traditions to try to achieve this. A synod's ruling may not be enough unless it is clearly seen to represent the consensus.

- Visual images are growing in importance and use. Some common language, form and rules should be developed both for pictures and for typography for those churches where some form of common identity is considered valuable. Style definitions for mainstream word processors may prove useful alongside published texts.

- Further resources are needed for the specific training of clergy and worship leaders both during initial training and through continuing ministerial education. The model of the Church of England's National Praxis Training Officer, part-funded through publishing income, might need repeating several times over.

Local church leaders whose churches are moving from the use of widely printed books to locally tailored worship material need to see the greater responsibility they are taking on themselves.

- Worship develops the whole worshipping community's spiritual formation. A local worship sheet does not just shape an event. The reasons for listening to the wider church go beyond what you should and should not do in a particular service.

- Worshippers often need ritual and routine in worship. Fresh service sheets every week may not just be wasteful, but confusing for those meeting them for the first time. The seasons of the year present a natural and widely owned rationale for the rhythm of liturgical change.

- We should not spend every working hour at a computer screen. Christ was about loving relationships and human interrelation.

- Engagement with the virtual world is something that local churches of all traditions are going to need to take on if the whole body of Christ is to be better made known. (Local churches should ask that the national church support this work through skills, resources and finance.)

- Beware! Church and copyright laws do exist, and normally for good reasons.

A Worship Sheet Check List
- Produce an outline to start with then fill in the texts.

- Consider printing only what is necessary and helpful for the congregation to follow and join in with the service. There are great advantages to keeping things down to four sides on one folded card. Normally all of the minister's words are not needed and if they are printed it may limit spontaneity and adjustment.

- If sources for a worship card come from a great library, it is difficult for the minister to hold this all in hand during a service. Print out any words for the leader not on the service card and put them in an A5 pocket book or bind them in some other way for convenience. If they are stored on the PC with the people's words, they will print out again should you call the service up again.

- If you have altered the line breaks for collects and prayers ask: was it really necessary and are the prayers still readable in a natural way?

- Proof read and spell check any freshly typed or scanned text. Beware 'The Cod of Israel praise.'

- Have you chosen appropriate typefaces? Sans serif typefaces tend to catch the eye well, serif typefaces are more easily read in dense blocks. Convention is serif fonts for reading text and sans serif reserved for headlines and posters. Although there are design reasons for ignoring this ministers should learn the rules before discovering when to break them.

- Pictures can help. Do yours? What do they say?

- Have you included the appropriate copyright notices?

- Discuss the draft with a worship committee or other representative group from the congregation—their comments should enhance things and may increase the willingness of all to feel a sense of ownership.

- If you are printing on to coloured paper (especially purple) is it light enough for those to read it whose sight is even more dim than your own?

- Do you need to provide some large print versions?

- Are any adaptations needed for a children's version?